REAL-LIFE
MONSTERS
SCALY, SLIPPERY
CREATURES

THE WORLD'S
WEIRDEST
REPTILES

Thanks to the creative team:
Senior Editor: Alice Peebles
Designer: Lauren Woods and collaborate agency

Original edition copyright 2015 by Hungry Tomato Ltd.

Hungry Tomato™
A division of Lerner Publishing Group, Inc.
241 First Avenue North
Minneapolis, MN 55401 USA

For reading levels and more information, look up this title
at www.lernerbooks.com.

Main body text set in Century Gothic Regular 9.5/11.5
Typeface provided by Monotype Corporation

Library of Congress Cataloging-in-Publication Data

Rake, Matthew, author.
    Scaly, slippery creatures / Matthew Rake ; Simon Mendez,
illustrator.
        pages cm. – (Real-life monsters)
        Summary: "Can you name the most poisonous snake on Earth?
Can you tell the difference between a Komodo dragon and a
crocodile? Meet some of the world's creepiest critters in this photo-
packed book of reptilian monsters" –Provided by publisher.
    Audience: Ages 8–12
    Audience: Grades 4 to 6
    ISBN 978-1-4677-6361-5 (lb : alk. paper)
    ISBN 978-1-4677-7645-5 (pb : alk. paper)
    ISBN 978-1-4677-7229-7 (eb pdf)
    1. Reptiles–Juvenile literature. 2. Poisonous snakes–Juvenile
literature. 3. Lizards–Juvenile literature. 4. Crocodiles–Juvenile
literature. I. Mendez, Simon, illustrator. II. Title.
QL644.2.R35 2016
597.9–dc23   2015012383

Manufactured in the United States of America
1 - VP - 7/15/15

REAL-LIFE
MONSTERS
SCALY, SLIPPERY
CREATURES

By Matthew Rake

Illustrated by Simon Mendez

HUNGRY
TOMATO™

Minneapolis

CONTENTS

Scaly, Slippery Creatures   6

Blood-Squirting Reptile Horned Lizard   8

Dressed To Frill Frilled Lizard   10

Angry If Alarmed Black Mamba   12

Pure Poison Inland Taipan   14

Monstrous Muncher Alligator Snapping Turtle   16

Fang-tastic Killer King Cobra   18

River Wrestler Water Monitor   20

Ruler of the River Nile Crocodile   22

Meat Seeker Komodo Dragon   24

The Big Daddy Saltwater Crocodile   26

Rogues' Gallery   28

Want to Know More?   30

Index   32

Reptiles have been on Earth for 315 million years—that's about 1,500 times longer than *Homo sapiens* have been around. In that time, reptiles have evolved into all sorts of animals, including crocodiles, lizards, snakes, and turtles. They live on land and in water all around the world, except in the very coldest climates.

So what are reptiles? They are vertebrates, which means they have backbones (yes, even snakes). They have scales. And they are cold-blooded, so they cannot control their own body heat. Reptiles need warmth from sunlight to become warm and active. And if they get too hot, they need to cool down by finding shade or water or burrowing underground. One big advantage of being cold-blooded is that reptiles don't need to eat a lot. Mammals consume food regularly to keep their body temperature up, but all reptiles have to do is kick back and soak up some rays. In fact, many reptiles—including crocodiles and snakes—can go for months without eating!

However, when reptiles do want a meal, they can be among the most ferocious animals on Earth. Crocodiles snap up anything they can get their jaws on. And once a crocodile has closed its jaws on an animal, those jaws are effectively locked. No creature can escape, not even a shark! Yes, that's right, some crocs will eat sharks!

Big lizards can be just as aggressive. When they are not killing animals to eat, they are fighting among themselves. Komodo dragons and water monitors hold bloody wrestling matches just to prove who is "top dog"—well, actually, "top lizard."

Smaller lizards may spend more time avoiding danger than creating it, but they still have weird and wonderful ways of protecting themselves. Take the horned lizard: it actually squirts blood from its eyes to scare off predators. And that works!

Snakes might not be as powerful as crocodiles or big lizards, but they can be just as lethal. In this book, you'll find out about the longest venomous snake in the world, the king cobra, and the most poisonous snake, the inland taipan. The venom from just one bite of an inland taipan can kill one hundred adult humans.

And let's not forget turtles. You might think that turtles are slow, gentle creatures. Well, you haven't met the alligator snapping turtle yet. It might be cold-blooded, but it is very hot-tempered.

If you're ready to meet some of the most belligerent creatures to walk the Earth, read on . . .

BLOOD-SQUIRTING REPTILE

HORNED LIZARD

Length: 1 - 8 in (2.5 - 20 cm)
Weight: 0.2 - 0.5 oz (5 - 15 g)
Location: North America

With its thick, tough, spiky skin, the horned lizard doesn't look like a particularly appetizing meal. But this squat, toadlike lizard is preyed upon by many animals, including snakes, coyotes, foxes, dogs, cats, wolves, and birds, including loggerhead shrikes, hawks and roadrunners. Since horned lizards are usually only a few inches long, you'd think they would be easy pickings for most of these animals. But they have evolved several ingenious ways to stay safe.

MASTER OF DISGUISE

Camouflage is the first line of defense that a horned lizard uses when a predator approaches. If this tactic doesn't work, some species employ one of the animal kingdom's most bizarre defenses: they squirt blood from their eyes directly at their foe, up to distances of 5 feet (1.5 meters). Scientists think the lizards do this by restricting the blood flow leaving the head, so the blood pressure increases and breaks open tiny blood vessels around the eyelids. It's meant to confuse would-be predators, but the blood also contains a chemical that is harmful or distasteful to dogs, wolves, and coyotes.

SIZE

1

POWER

2

STRENGTH

2

AGGRESSION

3

DEADLINESS

1

TOTAL

9

DRESSED TO FRILL

FRILLED LIZARD

Length: 3 ft (0.9 m)
Weight: up to 1 lb 2 oz (0.5 kg)
Location: northern Australia and
southern New Guinea

JUST FOR FRILLS

The frilled lizard gets its name from the pleated skin flap around its neck. When in danger, the lizard opens both the frill and its mouth to frighten its attacker. The frill is only about 1 foot (30 centimeters) across, but it is a startling sight, with the yellow or pink inside of the lizard's mouth showing between its gaping jaws. Even if this belligerent display does not work, it can buy the lizard enough time to turn tail—mouth and frill still open—and bolt for the nearest tree. It runs on its hind legs, with its upper limbs splayed and its head upright. This truly weird running action has earned it the name of bicycle lizard.

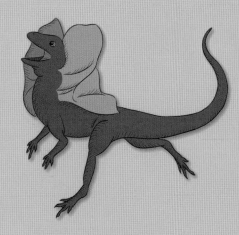

SIZE	2
POWER	3
STRENGTH	2
AGGRESSION	4
DEADLINESS	1
TOTAL	12

Although frilled lizards like to live in the safety of trees, the temptation of all those potential meals on the ground, especially spider ants and small lizards, is often just too much for them. On the ground, frilled lizards are liable to become prey themselves, to animals such as large lizards, snakes, dingoes and wild cats. This is where the frilled lizard's frill comes into play. It's a secret defense mechanism.

Length: up to 14 ft (4.5 m),
usually about 8 ft 2 in (2.5m)
Weight: about 3 lb 8 oz (1.6 kg)
Location: southern and eastern Africa

With its coffin-shaped head, lightning-fast reactions, and deadly bite, the black mamba is one of the world's most feared snakes. And for good reason: It is the second-longest venomous snake in the world, after the king cobra. What's more, the venom of a black mamba is not just highly toxic. It also works extremely quickly. It can kill an adult human in just 20 minutes.

DANGEROUS IF DISTURBED

The black mamba is the source of many myths and legends, including one that it will chase humans through forests! In fact, black mambas are shy, secretive, and usually try to avoid confrontation. One reason for the black mamba's "bad-boy" reputation is that it often lives among crops in fields and may attack farm workers who accidentally surprise it. When a black mamba senses danger, it is fast, nervous, and unpredictable.

BLACK HOLE

The black mamba is not actually black—it's olive gray. The snake is named after the inky black color inside its mouth, which it displays when threatened.

SIZE

4

POWER

6

STRENGTH

4

AGGRESSION

6

DEADLINESS

7

TOTAL

27

PURE POISON

INLAND TAIPAN

Length: up to 8 ft 2.5 in (2.5 m), usually about 6 ft 7 in (2 m)
Weight: 6 lb 10 oz (3 kg)
Location: central Australia

Australia's inland taipan is the most venomous snake in the world. The venom from one bite is estimated to be 68 times as poisonous as the king cobra's, and enough to kill 100 fully grown men. No wonder it is often called the "fierce snake." The good news is that the inland taipan has never been known to kill a human. In the rare cases that humans have been bitten, antivenom has been successful. Small rodents and birds, however, are not so lucky.

PURSUING ITS PREY

The inland taipan specializes in hunting mammals, so its venom is specially designed to kill warm-blooded species. Many venomous snakes strike with a single, accurate bite, then wait for the prey to die. But the inland taipan launches a series of rapid, accurate strikes. It can deliver eight venomous bites in a single attack, snapping its jaws several times to inflict multiple wounds. The venom acts so rapidly that the prey does not have time to fight back. Scientists have estimated that this snake injects more than 40,000 times the amount of venom needed to kill a 7-ounce (20 gram) rat.

SIZE
4

POWER
5

STRENGTH
4

AGGRESSION
7

DEADLINESS
9

TOTAL
29

6 MONSTROUS MUNCHER

ALLIGATOR SNAPPING TURTLE

Length (males): 16 - 32 in (40 - 80 cm)
Weight (males): 150 - 236 lb (68 - 107 kg)
Location: southeastern United States

This is one mean and moody reptile, and its name says it all. Surprisingly, it gets the alligator part of its name not from its aggression, but from the ridges on its shell, which look similar to an alligator's scales. And the snapping part? Well, that is due to its ferocious bite. If provoked, this turtle has been known to bite through broom handles easily and take human fingers completely off!

WAITING GAME

1 The alligator snapping turtle's hunting strategy is simple. It lies motionless at the bottom of murky rivers with its mouth wide open. Its grayish brown color helps it blend right into the mud, and the only part of its body that moves is the wormlike extension on its tongue.

2 When a curious fish comes to inspect this juicy morsel, the turtle snaps its mouth shut with lightning speed and brutal force.

3 Turtles can play the waiting game. They are able to stay submerged for 40 to 50 minutes before surfacing for air.

SIZE	7
POWER	4
STRENGTH	6
AGGRESSION	7
DEADLINESS	6
TOTAL	30

ROLL OFF THE TONGUE

The alligator snapping turtle has a body part that no other reptile has. On its tongue, it sports a bright red, worm-shaped piece of flesh. The alligator wiggles this extension to bait unsuspecting fish.

FANG-TASTIC KILLER

KING COBRA

Length: up to 18 ft 8 in (5.7 m)
usually 9 ft 11 in - 13 ft 1 in (3 - 4 m)
Weight: up to 28 lb (12.7 kg), usually 13 lb (6 kg)
Location: India and southeast Asia

The world's longest venomous snake, the king cobra, is a swift and ferocious hunter. It preys mainly on other snakes and occasionally on lizards and rodents. It detects prey through its forked tongue, which picks up scent particles and transfers them to a receptor in the roof of its mouth. It also senses vibrations in the earth and has very good eyesight: it can see moving prey from almost 330 feet (100 m) away.

FANG-TASTIC

When angered, the king cobra rears up, extending its neck, hissing loudly, and showing the two fangs at the front of its mouth. These hollow fangs inject venom into the prey, targeting the central nervous system and causing severe pain, blurred vision, and eventually paralysis. A bite from a king cobra can kill a human in as little as 30 minutes.

A REAL CHARMER

Snake charmers—such as this one (*right*) at a market in Marrakesh, Morocco—often use king cobras. Scientists think king cobras can't actually hear the charmer's music because, like all snakes, they don't have outer ears. Instead, they respond to the movement of the flute.

SIZE
6

POWER
6

STRENGTH
4

AGGRESSION
7

DEADLINESS
8

TOTAL
31

4 RIVER WRESTLER

WATER MONITOR

Length: up to 10 ft (3m);
usually 5 ft (1.5 m)
Weight: up to 100 lb (50 kg)
Location: south and southeast Asia

The water monitor will try to eat just about any other animal it encounters, including fish, frogs, rodents, birds, crabs, snakes, turtles, and even young crocodiles. Escaping one is no mean feat. It has powerful leg muscles for a quick turn of speed on land. And, as its name suggests, this reptile feels at home in the water. Propelled by its long powerful tail, the water monitor is a strong swimmer and can pursue prey underwater for 30 minutes or more.

If there is no live prey available, water monitors will eat carrion, or meat from dead animals. They are also big egg eaters. They raid birds' nests to dig up turtle and crocodile eggs.

Not many animals prey on water monitors. Saltwater crocs will try, of course. (They'll try to attack anything!) Large snakes, such as reticulated pythons or king cobras, sometimes also go after small specimens. However, water monitors are nimble movers and can climb trees to escape, jumping from branch to branch to reach safety.

SIZE

6

POWER

8

STRENGTH

6

AGGRESSION

8

DEADLINESS

6

TOTAL

34

A RUCKUS IN THE RIVER

Male water monitors wrestle to establish who is the bigger shot in the river, especially if they are both after the same female. Like a pair of sumo wrestlers, they stand up on their hind legs and grapple. These reptile fights are bloodier than sumo wrestling, though. Each lizard grips its opponent with its forelegs and uses its claws to rake vivid pink gashes in its rival's back. The fights can last much longer than a sumo wrestling match too. If one lizard topples, it often twists back and resecures its grip on its foe. It can take 30 minutes before one admits defeat and slinks away.

RULER OF THE RIVER
RIVER
NILE CROCODILE

Length: up to 20 ft (6 m); usually 16 ft (5m)
Weight: up to 2000 lb (900 kg);
usually 660 lb (300 kg)
Location: Africa, south of the Sahara

Cunning and immensely powerful, Nile crocodiles terrorize the rivers of Africa. They lurk patiently beneath the surface near riverbanks, keeping just their eyes and nostrils clear of the water, so they can breathe and keep watch without being seen. Just about any animal that comes for a drink is in danger, and when a crocodile sees a likely victim, it moves silently forward underwater before lunging out of the water in a lethal attack.

THE DEATH ROLL

Nile crocodiles have an extremely powerful bite and sharp conical teeth. Once they get a grip on an animal, it is almost impossible to loosen— even for a creature as large as this wildebeest (*right*).

When the prey is dead, the croc rips off and swallows huge chunks of flesh. Often, with big prey such as a wildebeest or a zebra, lots of crocs will work together, using each other for leverage, and then share the spoils. One croc bites down hard, while another performs the "death roll," violently spinning its body to tear off the meat.

SIZE

9

POWER

8

STRENGTH

8

AGGRESSION

10

DEADLINESS

9

TOTAL

44

2 MEAT SEEKER

KOMODO DRAGON

Length: up to 10 ft 3 in (3.13 m)
Weight: up to 366 lb (166 kg)
Location: southeast Indonesia

The heaviest, strongest, and deadliest lizard in the world, the Komodo dragon attacks with long powerful claws, large serrated teeth, and a huge powerful tail. And for defense, it has a covering of armored scales that contain bony plates known as osteoderms.

Komodo dragons threaten every animal they come in contact with–living or dead! They regularly eat deer, pigs, smaller Komodo dragons, birds, water buffalo, and fish. Given the chance, they will also eat humans! If they can't find a live human, they are quite happy to dig one up from a shallow grave. Luckily, for the rest of us in the animal kingdom, the Komodo dragon lives only on five islands in Indonesia in southeastern Asia.

The Komodo dragon's hunting strategy is based on stealth and patience, ambushing its prey rather than pursuing it over long distances. It kills small animals right away, but with large ones—such as the water buffalo below—it is prepared to play a waiting game. The lizard wounds the buffalo with a bite or two, then lets the toxic bacteria in its saliva poison the buffalo's blood. One study estimated that this reptile's saliva contains 57 different strains of bacteria. And some scientists think the dragon also possesses a venom that stops the victim's blood from clotting and leads to paralysis.

Either because of the saliva or the venom or both, the buffalo eventually weakens and dies. It may take hours or even days, but the Komodo dragon will eventually get its dinner.

SIZE

8

POWER

9

STRENGTH

9

AGGRESSION

10

DEADLINESS

9

TOTAL

45

25

1 THE BIG DADDY

SALTWATER CROCODILE

Length: up to 23 ft (7 m); usually 14 ft 9 in (4.5 m)
Weight: up to 3,300 lb (1,500 kg);
usually 1,100 lb (500 kg)
Location: southeast Asia, north Australia

Salties are the largest crocodiles and, according to many scientists, the most aggressive. The saltwater crocodile is not a fussy eater. You name it, it eats it, and that even includes sharks. In 2014, for instance, in Kakadu National Park in Australia, an 18 foot (5.5 m) male known as Brutus was photographed eating a bull shark (*right*). Brutus, who is about 80 years old, is missing a front leg, and guides at the park think it was probably bitten off by a bull shark. So maybe Brutus got his revenge.

A CARING SIDE

Saltwater crocs are very good parents. The mother makes a nest out of a mound of plants and mud. She breaks off the vegetation with her teeth and scrapes everything together with her hind legs.

SIZE
10

POWER
8

STRENGTH
9

AGGRESSION
10

DEADLINESS
9

TOTAL
46

HORNED LIZARD

The horned lizard lives in dry climates and has a great way of making use of all the rainwater that falls. It raises its tail, lowers its head, and lets the rain run in narrow channels down its back—and right into its mouth.

FRILLED LIZARD

Besides defense, this lizard's colorful frill may be used to help attract potential mates and to help control its body temperature— opening the frill creates more surface area to absorb heat.

ALLIGATOR SNAPPING TURTLE

The only safe way to grasp the turtle's shell is just behind its head and in front of the tail. But you'll need some muscle because it's a heavyweight. Its only rival as the largest freshwater turtle is the Yangtze giant softshell turtle.

KING COBRA

After biting its victim, the king cobra starts to swallow its struggling prey while toxins begin digesting its victim. Like all snakes, it has flexible jaws. This allows it to swallow prey whole, including animals much larger than its head.

KOMODO DRAGON

The Komodo dragon is really a type of monitor lizard, so why is it called a dragon? Well, its fierce nature, yellowish color, and long, forked tongue reminded people of the mythical dragons that spit fire! And the Komodo part? That's one of the five islands it lives on in Indonesia.

BLACK MAMBA

The black mamba often climbs trees to prey on birds, and it has perfect camouflage to do so. From above, its olive-gray color makes it look like another branch. From below, the snake blends into the sky because of its light underbelly.

INLAND TAIPAN

The inland taipan was first described by Frederick McCoy in 1879 and then by William John Macleay in 1882. For the next 90 years, no more specimens were found, and it was completely forgotten until a tour operator was bitten in 1967.

WATER MONITOR

Some water monitors have been seen eating catfish in the same way mammals do. They tear off chunks of meat with their sharp teeth while holding the catfish with their forelegs, which allows them to rip off parts of the fish.

NILE CROCODILE

At night, the Nile crocodile has been known to hunt on land, ambushing prey near forest trails. The crocs have very good night vision and are capable of briefly reaching speeds of 7.5 - 9 miles per hour (12 - 14 km/h).

SALTWATER CROCODILE

Baby salties weigh only 2.5 ounces (70 g), and scientists estimate that only 1 in 100 survive to become adults. If a lucky one grows to reach 1,543 pounds (700 kg), as many saltwater crocs do, it will be 10,000 times heavier than it was at birth. Compare that with humans: on average, a newborn baby weighs 7.5 pounds (3.4 kg) and an adult weighs 137 pounds (62 kg)—that's only about 18 times heavier.

BLACK MAMBA

Not many animals prey on the black mamba, for obvious reasons! But one animal that is certainly not scared of the creature is the secretary bird. Although the bird can fly, it prefers to hunt on the ground, using its fearsome, swordlike talons as weapons. It kicks and claws the black mamba to death, safe in the knowledge that the thick scales on its legs will protect it against the snake's lethal bite. Snake eagles also have this protection. They usually swoop down behind a black mamba, then crush its head with their talons and beak. Other animals that take their chances with the black mamba include the mongoose (see "King Cobra," *below*) and the cape file snake, which preys on other snakes, including small black mambas.

KING COBRA

In one of the stories in Rudyard Kipling's *Jungle Stories*, Rikki-Tikki-Tavi, a brave young pet mongoose, protects its owners from two big bad cobras, who go by the names of Nag and Nagaina. If you believe that's just a made-up story, think again. Kipling was born in India and he knew the mongoose was one animal that was definitely not afraid of the king cobra. The mongoose has a thick coat to protect it against the cobra's bite and is immune to its venom. What's more, it is amazingly quick and agile. It usually jumps and ducks away from the snake's hissing attacks, waiting for a chance to get one firm bite behind the cobra's head. Then the snake is a goner.

ALLIGATOR SNAPPING TURTLE

These turtles mate in spring and the female lays a clutch of between eight and 50 eggs about two months later. She puts the eggs in a nest she has dug in the sand about 160 feet (50 m) from the water. The eggs hatch in the fall, and the tiny turtles are only about 2 inches (5 cm) long. Their sex is dependent on how hot it has been. If the eggs reach about 84-86°F (29-30°C), the turtles are likely to be all female. If it's any cooler, they will probably be males.

SALTWATER CROCODILE

The longest saltie ever measured was called Lolong, who was 20 feet 3 inches (6.17 m). He was caught in Bunawan Creek in the Philippines in 2011, because he was believed to have killed a fisherman and a 12-year-old girl. The hunters set four traps, which Lolong destroyed. They then used sturdier traps with steel cables, one of which finally caught the enormous reptile. About 100 people had to pull the crocodile, which weighed about 2,370 pounds (1,075 kg), from the creek to a clearing where a crane lifted it into a truck. Lolong became the star attraction of an ecotourism park in Bunawan until he died in 2013.

KOMODO DRAGON

After mating, the female Komodo dragon usually lays her eggs in burrows abandoned by the orange-footed scrubfowl. This bird builds nests out of leaves, and the heat from the decomposing leaves is perfect for incubating the Komodo dragon's eggs.

INDEX

alligator snapping turtle, 16–17, 28, 31

black mamba, 12–13, 29, 30
Brutus, 26

camouflage, 9, 17, 29
characteristics of reptiles, 6
cold-blooded reptiles, 6
crocodiles, 6–7
    baby, 27, 29
    nests, 27
    Nile crocodile, 22–23, 29
    saltwater crocodile, 26–27, 29, 31

death roll, 23

eating habits, 6

frilled lizard, 10–11, 28

horned lizard, 8–9, 28

inland taipan, 14–15, 29

king cobra, 18–19, 28, 30
Kipling, Rudyard, 30
Komodo dragon, 24–25, 28, 31

lizards, 7
    frilled lizard, 10–11, 28
    horned lizard, 8–9, 28
    Komodo dragon, 24–25, 28, 31
    water monitor, 7, 20–21, 29
Lolong, 31

mongoose, 30

Nile crocodile, 22–23, 29

saltwater crocodile, 26–27, 29, 31
secretary bird, 30
snake charmers, 19
snake eagle, 30
snakes, 7
    black mamba, 12–13, 29, 30
    inland taipan, 14–15, 29
    king cobra, 18–19, 28, 30
    venom, 12, 14–15, 18

turtles, 7
    alligator snapping turtle, 16–17, 28, 31

water monitor, 7, 20–21, 29

THE AUTHOR
Matthew Rake lives in London, England, and has worked in publishing for more than twenty years. He has written on a wide variety of topics including science, sports, and the arts.

THE ARTIST
Award-winning illustrator Simon Mendez combines his love of nature and drawing by working as an illustrator with a focus on scientific and natural subjects. He paints a wide variety of themes but mainly concentrates on portraits and animal subjects. He lives in the United Kingdom.

Picture Credits (abbreviations: t = top; b = bottom; c = center; l = left; r = right)

© www.shutterstock.com: 5 br, 7br, 9bl, 13 tr, 16b, 20, bl, 23 tr, 25 tr, 27 tr, 28tl, 30 cl, 30 cr, 30b, 31 tl, 31 cl, 20 b, 31 tr, 31 cl, 31 br.

19 tr, Cobra in Market Place: Philip Lange / Shutterstock.com